My Spiritual Journey
A Guide to Self Discovery

PEGGY HALL FLAGG

Copyright © 2016 Peggy Hall Flagg

All rights reserved.

ISBN-13 978-0692797020 (Silver Pegasus Publishing)
ISBN-10 978-0692797025

ACKNOWLEDGMENTS

I would like to thank my mentors for sharing and inspiring me to take a deeper look at possibilities: F. Coll, Jill Turner/Tushwa, Rene Avery and Ahura Z. Diliiza.

I'd also like to acknowledge my husband for all the backing both emotionally and financially as I went on my journey. I am very grateful for him for accepting a steady stream of leaders that stayed at our house. He never minded my traveling as long as he didn't have to be involved. The mold was broken when he passed on.

And finally, I want to thank the many like-minded souls I have met along the way. May your journey be smooth and fulfilling.

During these times it is important to pray.

Pray for yourself.

Pray for the election, that the person elected is God-led.

Pray for the government to be God-centered and remember they are representing their constituents.

Above all, pray for world peace.

Prayer is important. When two or more are gathered in His name. I have seen a group move mountains. Through prayer anything is possible!

CONTENTS

1	My Beginnings	1
2	My Spiritual Journey	13
3	The Chakras	19
4	Healing	25
5	Creating	29
6	Our Senses and More	33
7	Reincarnation	37
8	You Are Unique	45
9	Dimensions	49
10	Meditation/Communication	53
11	Miscellaneous Tidbits	57

1. MY BEGINNINGS

As I look at it, my whole life has been on a spiritual path.

I was born on Quaker Ridge in Casco, Maine. Just to look out our kitchen window was an inspiration to life itself; one of the most beautiful views overlooking many mountains and lakes. The view was always changing and the sunsets were different every evening. It seemed as if the sunset was always trying to be more beautiful than the night before. It always inspired me.

My father was a mortician and my mother a housewife who oversaw the needs of the family (a fabulous cook she was!). I had two brothers; one a year older and one a year younger, and I was wedged in the middle. As a middle child I felt people didn't notice me. The baby usually gets the attention and the oldest is trying cute new things. Somehow I felt I just existed alone. Is that how all middle children feel, especially those so close in age? Maybe it was because I was a girl.

Since the funeral chapel was attached to the house there was quite a bit of activity I sensed. I remember once as I was falling asleep and was in that alpha stage, I heard footsteps coming up the stairs. It stopped at my room, the first room at the top of the stairs. I looked up and this man looked at me. I pulled the blankets over my head and froze in place and could not move. I could hear him go in the bathroom, turn on the water and then go downstairs. I didn't want to see any more souls that had passed on. Of course, I didn't dare tell anyone as they might think I was losing my mind and I wasn't so sure of myself.

A few other experiences like that and my interest was stimulated so I wanted to delve deeper into the paranormal field.

After a few years of involvement in the metaphysical I could see why I chose the family I did for growth. I believe a mortician for a father made me more curious about death and the afterlife. I didn't get answers from him that were satisfying because he thought death was very final. I had the feeling that there had to be more. It didn't make sense to me to be born, go to school, have a job, raise a family and then transition and that was it!

As I looked back I needed some masculine energy from my brothers. I had been a female in many of the last incarnations and I needed more balance in my life. I needed to learn to be physically stronger and tougher. Since the few children in the neighborhood were boys, if I wanted to be involved in their game playing I had to learn basketball, baseball and all the like things they were doing. I turned into quite an athlete myself!

When I was fourteen a cousin brought some books to our house. Included among them was a book about a person being hypnotized to go back into her childhood, but what she shared during her hypnotic sessions was herself in other lifetimes as different people. I read and reread that book several times and was very fascinated with reincarnation. I just knew I had lived as another person before. Thus, I started my conscious journey to find out more about my soul and where I had traveled and lived.

Actually, my childhood from when I was born until five years of age is pretty much a blur. When I was five my older brother was attending school, which was just out the road from our house. I was at the age that I wanted to go to school also but was too young. However, at recess time I would go over and play with some of the children and sometimes the teacher would invite me to stay for the afternoon and I was always excited about going to big school.

The next year when I was old enough to attend school they closed that school and I attended another with eight classes in one room (this was in Casco Village and we had cadet teachers. They were going to college but practiced teaching at small schools). World War II was going strong then and my father was drafted. He had basic training here in the states and then was shipped to Japan.

Everyone was experiencing hardships but we were some of the lucky ones as we lived on a small farm and raised our own food. We always had plenty to eat with all the canned goods. Our root cellar was full of apples, potatoes, carrots, beets and salt pork soaking in brine for traditional Saturday night beans. We also raised pigs, beef cattle, chickens, cows for milk and bees for honey.

On the farm there was always plenty of work to do. There was planting, weeding and harvesting crops. Every year came picking rocks from the garden soil before planting (I thinks rocks were born--they certainly multiplied each year!). Each season brought its own tasks to be done. Hay season was always a big thing as my father and a friend bought a hay baler and other equipment jointly and we had other farms that we hayed. Haying was always fun for me because all I had to do was drive the tractor and rake the hay into rows for the baler to come by. I thought I was quite a professional driver at eleven!

With autumn came bringing the wood, which had been drying for a year, into the wood shed for the winter.

I had a pet peeve. For two years my father and his friend, Richard Frank, planted three or four acres of pickling cucumbers. Each morning during the growing season we would be in the garden picking the really small cucumbers. We would fill a dump truck body full and then they would take them to the factory in Oxford. This was about a five-hour day job seven days a week. I would protest but it was no good. My being a girl didn't excuse me from work! The things I flat-out refused to do however was chop a chicken's head off and pull the insides out, but I did pluck them. The other thing I wouldn't do was milk a cow (how I got out of that I don't know!).

The rest of my schooling was in Webb's Mills and then Casco Memorial School was built and I attended there from fourth through eighth grades.

I loved high school and all the activities, especially sports. It's a time of fun with all the friends; boys and girls. We went to the movies and my favorite activity was roller skating. Otherwise we created our own entertainment. I think our telephone on a party line was our only real technology--no wonder it's mostly a mystery to me now!

All this time I was asking myself, "What is my purpose in life, what am I to do?".

One of my closest friends and I were what we called "psychic" because we could actually read each others minds. Sometimes it took just one word out of one mouth and the other would finish the sentence.

I had applied, was tested and had been accepted to Maine Medical School of Nursing for further education. My mother was a caretaker of those in the family who were sick and old. She thought it would be a great idea if I was a nurse and that's how I decided. Back in the fifties the profession choices for a girl was to be a nurse, secretary or teacher and that was about it. I took the college course in school so wasn't trained as a secretary.

At that time the nursing school was a dorm and system by itself. Not through a college like today. I was in the first class that lived and attended the study part at the old Maine Eye and Ear Infirmary that closed and was refurbished into a dorm and classrooms. The administration and teachers were very strict and I wasn't used to that. Rebellion set in and I was always on the wrong side of the door.

Well, to make a long story short, I didn't like nursing. The smells and sight of vomit made me sick (though blood didn't bother me). I really disliked everything about it and decided this path was not for me.

My friend, Janet, from high school and I got an apartment in Portland and I worked in a bank in the bookkeeping department. The bookkeeping machines were a big contraption that made lots of noise (no computers then!). I worked there and all the time I was trying to decide what to do and what my purpose was. I always knew what it wasn't by process of elimination but not what would be fulfilling. I was thinking of going to the University of Maine to be a physical education teacher. I had already passed the entrance exam when I was a junior in high school and my high school principal took an interest and took me to Orono for a visit because he thought I'd make a good sports coach. My older brother was a freshman there.

I was dating my future husband Jim while in nursing school and my time in Portland. He was a senior at SMVTI in South Portland. Somehow I wasn't sure about college and we decided to get married before I was to go. We married on the fourth of July. I said it was my independence day.

Jim worked at Flagg Lumber Company and I continued to work at the bank in Portland and drove back and forth every day until just before Christmas when the snow was starting to pile up. In March we moved into our new house that was being built. That was a fun time. Then the babies started coming. Tamra, our first, was twenty months old when Terry, the second child was born. I was a stay-at-home mother. Our son Todd didn't come until six years later.

I worked in the summers when all the summer businesses opened. I usually worked around restaurants, either as a waitress, short-order cook, prep cook, cashier or whatever was needed. One summer a friend, Nancy and I leased a place and served lobsters.

Life was busy as the children grew and went to school. They were all good kids and no big issues with them. There were always their friends around and a swimming pool in the backyard kept them busy during the summer.

All this time I was still wondering what my blueprint was. I was reading anything I could find that had to do with self-understanding and the psychic world. At that time, in the late sixties, the only books I could find were about Edgar Cayce. He was the "sleeping prophet" who, while in a deep trance would answer a person's questions and worked with those who were ill. He would give a remedy for healing. I read everything I could find about him.

About that time I met a new friend, Jackie, who was interested in the same field and we would get together and discuss things we had read. After the children were off to school we would visit or call one another every day to discuss the spiritual things.

She had three children as I did and they were friendly so our families were together a lot. We had many potluck dinners by cleaning out our refrigerators. Our husbands also shared some interests.

One April school vacation our two families planned a trip to Virginia Beach and Jackie and I spent a lot of time at Edgar Cayce's Association of Research and Enlightenment. It was a beautiful library and I'm sure it has expanded since 1970. There were a few beds there where people would come and stay like a hospital to have Edgar's remedies applied. I did see his son, Hugh Lynn, walking around at one time. His work is still being studied (interestingly Edgar Cayce's birthday was March 18, the same day as my own and my mentor Ahura Z. It is said the same birthday means the same vibrational frequency).

The trip wasn't just for us though. We took a tour of Norfolk Naval Base where John was stationed while in the navy. We also went to Williamsburg Virginia for a little education for the children.

Many good times were had with the Schrader family including trips, snowmobile Sundays and Jackie and I on our motorcycles. We discovered the Inner Peace Movement and became involved in that self-development/metaphysical program. We were so excited to find something that shared the same beliefs that we went to Atlanta, Georgia for leadership training. That was the beginning of my journey.

For the next twenty years I was involved in the program. Many weekends there was a course held in Salisbury, Pennsylvania where the affiliated college was located. I can't count the trips I made and many times I went by myself for the fifteen hour drive. Jackie was involved for a while and then went on to other things. Unfortunately she transitioned quite a few years ago and I still think of her with love.

I would attend anything remotely in the field of the psychic and self-discovery. One time I went to Boston for a weekend because J. Z. Knight was going to be there and she channeled a soul named Ramtha. At that time I was suffering with a hip and joint issue. I was in pain most of the time and all the doctors I went to couldn't find anything wrong. During the session on the last day Ramtha came to me and lifted up my leg, rubbed the calf, looked on the bottom of my foot and said "this body has too much yeast". I had never heard of such a thing and my friend from Belfast was there and said she had just had a book on yeast come into her book shop and would send it to me. After going on the eating regime the book suggested and with some medicine from the doctor I was healed of the pain that had been with me for a couple of years.

My involvement took me all over New England along with things in Nova Scotia. I lead groups and taught classes for those twenty years. Sometimes I was out three nights a week traveling from home. I often went to Pennsylvania to teach courses at the colleges. The founder of the Inner Peace Movement was originally from Puerto Rico and still owned a house in San Juan. Every year in February he would offer a classes and I attended a couple of times.

I met a lot of people and formed some great relationships, all of like mind. After twenty years I decided to try other things although I wasn't sure where I was headed, but I knew that whatever I wanted to tell the Universe and it would be provided as long as it took me in the right direction.

2. MY PATH

After I left the Inner Peace Movement, I formed local groups to share some of the wisdom I had gained from years of study that had become a part of me. I continued teaching and leading groups for a year or so and all the time I was still searching for more answers.

I understood that the more I know the more there is to know. I don't think there is ever an end to learning about the planets and different areas we travel and "live". There are many of things to explore.

I was invited out to New Mexico through a friend to attend a channeling session at the home of Jamie Sams. A friend from Connecticut and I flew out for a visit and explored the area. Jamie lived in the mountains in the outskirts of Santa Fe and is a Native American of the Cherokee and Seneca tribes.

I had a real enjoyable evening. We all brought food to share for the potluck dinner. There were about twenty of us there and we got to explore her grounds. In the back there was a separate building where she did massage and some of her work. I was impressed with all the Katrina Dolls she had made and displayed in her living room. I asked where she got her blue refrigerator as I had never seen one. She had taken it to a car body shop to have it painted.

Jamie is a very talented woman and has written several books along with The Medicine Cards and co-wrote The Sacred Path Cards all based on Native American beliefs.

A place in Maine I find interesting is the Wilhelm Reich museum in Rangely Maine. Dr. Reich was a psychoanalyst from Austria and a refugee from Germany. He was in Freud's inner circle and made many discoveries such as orgone energy (which is life energy), cloud busters, and he developed therapeutic methods to help people with their suppressed emotions.

He was misrepresented and a lot of his work was destroyed. He was not appreciated for his discoveries and work he had done. He was put in jail and transitioned there. A trip to Rangely to the museum is an education where you can attend movies or talks and buy books and papers on his work.

The next phase of my journey began with a telephone call from a friend in Washington DC. She was inviting me to her home to meet a spiritual lady from New Mexico who gave readings and counselings. I went to the session and was hooked.

Rene held four-day classes in New Mexico at least once a year and we had conference calls at least twice a week and sometimes more. She also formed a special group of ten who met twice a year to work on special projects. Sometimes she brought a person's higher self in to talk with us. I do remember the current presidents of the time and I especially remember George senior when George W. was running for president--he said he'd do anything to get his son elected and he did.

Another time I remember taking a soul trip to the Vatican when the Illuminate was meeting there. I remember seeing a lot of well known souls. They were up to no good with their plans and still are.

I flew to New Mexico twice a year for ten years. Rene lived in Taos and moved to Lake Cochiti between Albuquerque and Santa Fe. There were four women from New England who belonged to the group and we decided to drive out once. It was a learning experience for four women in a car for four long days!

I drove out by myself once and stayed with Rene for six weeks. We took some day trips and she held a course while I was there. We went to the casino a few times (she called it "golfing" and asked me if I wanted to go golfing!). I spent a lot of time with her husband as Rene was busy giving readings as that was her income. He took me to different places around that were of interest. We went to Los Alamos, one of his pet peeves, where there is a nuclear lab and lots of nuclear weapons are stored.

While there, a friend invited me to go to a ranch in California to bring back two zebus to her home in Taos. While in California Carolyn took me to Yosemite National Park, Pebble Beach golf course where I had to call my now pro-golfer grandson.

While this was all going on I was still teaching groups locally and held some classes at a metaphysical book store in Portland (Rene is no longer with us and I want to thank her for all the wisdom she passed on to me and others. She was also a great friend and I miss her).

I attend new and different programs and classes I hear about. Braco is special to me right now. He stands in front of his audience, gazes into their eyes and often a healing takes place. I have been in his presence four times, in Connecticut, Boston and twice in New Jersey. The first time I looked into his eyes I felt an electric bolt go through my chest (I guess something in my heart needed adjusting). I also felt a pain in my knee and that was much better. Other times I felt better and always a great peace within.

He is from Croatia and has a place in Hawaii so he spends time in each place. Every month or two he holds a three day program on the internet live streaming. I find his presence on live streaming is very healing also. Just Google "Braco".

Another thing that means a lot to me is my relationship with Tom Tam and the people that work with him. Tom is a refugee from China and now has an international program on acupuncture. I took some courses from him in the Boston area--not how to do acupuncture but an understanding of the process. If I feel something in my body I want fixed I go for a session in Haverhill where he has a healing room. It's as simple as unblocking blocked energy that causes the discomfort of pain.

I now have a new mentor here in Maine, Ahura Z. Diliiza, and he has the depth of wisdom and understand I need to continue growing. I am very thankful for him and his guidance. He runs a school of metaphysics in Standish and teaches private classes through the internet to people all over the world.

This book contains some of the basic things I have learned along the way and I want to share them with those interested in the field of metaphysics and maybe inspire others by letting them know that there is a lot more in the universe to learn and experience than meets the eye.

3. THE CHAKRAS

The chakras are an interesting study as they can reveal a lot about physical, mental, emotional and spiritual energies and how it relates to aspects of our consciousness.

Chakra is a Sanskrit word that means "wheel". The chakras spin like a wheel and they spin clockwise if they are in balance. There are hundreds of chakras in the body and seven main ones in the physical body where there is a concentration of energy that corresponds to one of the glands of the endocrine system. There are five outside the body in the etheric field that has to do with our connection to the universe.

Energy flows throughout our physical body and the chakras receive and send the energy. Thinking affects the flow of energy. When we are very emotional or have negative thoughts it blocks the flow of energy and we experience the block as pain, aches, bruises or discomfort in some way.

The bottom three chakras have to do with us on planet Earth and the grounding needed to survive and feel you belong here. The top four starting with the heart have to do with our connection to the universe.

All energy centers have a color associated with them. Starting at the bottom and going up, the chakras follow the colors of the rainbow. Each chakra has a musical note associated with it, starting with middle C and going up to high C.

Many physical issues can be diagnosed when we know what the chakra represents.

The first chakra is located at the base of the spine and is called the root or coccyx chakra. This chakra has to do with wants and the physical energy in your body. If you are experiencing discomfort in the lower back or down the legs, what is it you want and don't have. The color is red and the corresponding musical note is middle C.

An example of how the wants work; I know a person who had no direction in her life and was searching and trying many different things. She was having a very hard and painful time with sciatica. All it took was someone to ask her if she could do anything what would it be and a similar avenue was available without her going back to school for training. When she made that decision of what she wanted to do with her life the pain left and never again did she experience discomfort in that area.

Another example was my daughter. There was going to be a middle school dance and she asked her father for a new outfit. He said no, that she had many things she could wear. The following morning she had a terrible backache and refused to go to school. I knew how much she must be focusing on her want of a new outfit and told her to get ready and we would go to the city and find something she would like to wear. Her backache stopped and no more complaints. It was that simple to heal her.

The second chakra is the reproductive chakra. This gland has to do with needs. It is to make sure our basic needs are met. The needs are health, food, home, love and sex. If a need is out of balance or denied then there may be issues in the reproductive, urinary tract, spleen and kidney area. It is necessary to meet these needs to heal the discomfort. The color associated with this chakra is orange and the musical note is D.

The third chakra is the solar plexus and has to do with our identification and mental energy, willpower and control over ourselves. It's our beliefs and thoughts. An out-of-balance solar plexus can mean trouble with the stomach, liver, digestion and small intestine. Yellow is the color of this chakra and the musical note is E.

An example could be if you are going to meet someone and you don't feel completely comfortable your stomach may have cramps or feel nervous. Having these different feelings doesn't throw your chakra out of balance just experiencing it briefly but thoughts you play over and over like a broken record is when issues may appear.

The heart chakra is the fourth chakra and has to do with drive and incentive in life to be of service. It has to do with enthusiasm to get involved with projects you want to accomplish. It has to do with love, compassion and forgiveness. The thymus, lungs, blood pressure, lymph system and of course the heart are all a part of the fourth chakra. Stress is a large factor in having or not having the heart function properly. This gland energizes the physical body. The color of this chakra is green with pink (love) around it. The musical note is F on the musical scale.

The fifth chakra is the thyroid chakra that is located in the throat area. It includes the thyroid, neck, ears, nose and sinus. This chakra is the relating and expression gland. It is the ability to feel relaxed and comfortable in all situations when sharing with people and listening to their opinions. It is expressing your thoughts and feelings and remaining calm. Blue is the color associated with this chakra and the musical note is G.

I am telling you the color associated with each chakra because you can use the color to heal the area and also eat the color food that goes with that chakra (more on this in the Healing chapter).

If you have a sore throat it is usually that you have difficulty relating to a person or a situation. I have heard a person on the telephone and they cough every few words.

This is because they are having a difficult time communicating.

The sixth chakra is called the pituitary gland or brow chakra and includes the hypothalamus, nervous system, eyes and brain. It is located behind the forehead and is also known as the third eye. This is our inner television screen. The center of outflow and giving and the sharing part of us. The color associated with this gland is purple and the note is A.

The seventh is the pineal or crown chakra. It is located at the base of the skull where the spinal column begins. It is the connection to our source in the universe. It has to do with compassion, oneness and harmony. It also has to do with self-acceptance. Many times a person will have an ache in the back of the neck and down into the shoulders. This could be the person is putting themselves down for not feeling adequate, not being attractive enough, intelligent enough or some negative thought about not measuring up. The color vibration of this gland is white and the note is B.

I have given a thumbnail sketch of the glands but there are so many things to learn as to what causes illness in our body and how our thoughts affect us. If you change your thoughts you change the energy in the body.

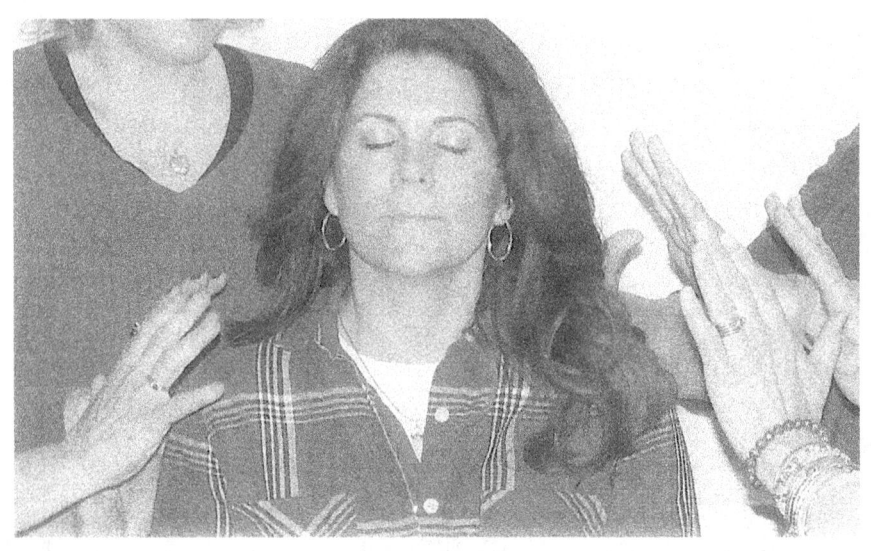

This lady is receiving some healing energy.

4. HEALING

When the body is functioning in good health, energy flows through the physical body without interruption. When our thinking is out of balance then we cause a block to occur and we experience discomfort of some kind.

An example of this might be having a disagreement with the spouse. If you keep thinking about it you probably will develop a sore throat or cold. Change your mind or see things differently so you feel peaceful about the situation.

Stress is the biggest cause of blocks in the body. Is anything really worth the pressure we put on ourselves? Relax and enjoy the world around you. We were meant to enjoy, have fun, be happy and love!

Attitude is everything. The biggest healing one can have is to change the concept.

There are many alternative ways of healing. I personally think that acupuncture is a great method of opening up the blocks to let the energy flow through the body. There are also many things you can do to heal the energy in your body. One is the laying on of hands. Usually it works better to have another person so you can work on each other. You can pound energy into the area without touching.

Using color can help by using the color of the chakra I have mentioned. Depending on the area needing healing will dictate which color to use. Green is always a good healing color as is pink for love--usually if we are having an issue with a certain area it's because we don't love ourselves enough. Send love to that area and tell it how much you love that particular place on your body.

Eating certain foods also helps. Eat the color food that corresponds with the chakra. If it's heart issues eat green vegetables. For circulation use the color red, beets are good.

Crystals are a great healing source. This is a study in itself, but the laying on of crystals is very healing. Playing of the crystal bowls in another healing method. You can buy the bowls but they are fairly expensive if you purchase the larger ones. Some people offer sessions with the bowls and usually you can find this at a metaphysical store. There is a bowl that represents each chakra by vibration and when they play that bowl it resonates and stimulates the energy there. This is something like the certain keys of the piano that corresponds with each chakra because it is the same vibration.

I have a friend in New Mexico who heals with crystals. She does this remotely and has had great response. She has at least a million dollars worth of crystals. Most of them came from temples in Tibet when the Chinese took over the area. These crystals were smuggled out of the country and many ended up in the US. She had connections to be the owner of them and has made a study as to what properties each contains. She programs them with intentions for what she wants to accomplish.

Crystals come in all shapes and sizes. Friends in New Mexico have a one ton Shiva Lingam in their front yard which is egg shaped. I have one the size of a thimble. These sacred stones come from the Narmada River in India and to my knowledge is the only place found. This stone relates and is healing to the heart chakra. In the movie of Indiana Jones and the Temple of Doom they were looking for the sacred stone and Shiva Lingam was what they were searching for.

There are many other healing modalities available; massage, Reiki, EFT, Reconnection Technique, Healing Code, reflexology and on and on. New methods are always being created. You need to use what feels good to you. Many times it is mind over matter.

The greatest healing one can have is the healing of concepts. Our mind is a great asset in helping us through life but it can also be our worst enemy depending on how we program and create with it.

Preparing for a technique.

5. CREATING

Planet earth is the creative planet of the universe.

We create all the time with our thoughts because energy follows thoughts. In other words, thoughts become things. Every thought has a frequency so if you think about something over and over it will materialize--good or bad.

We are human transmission towers. Thoughts are sent out into the universe and they magnetically attract all like things that are of the same frequency. Everything sent out returns to the source--you. This is the same way we attract the people we do. We are a magnet and like attracts like.

If you can visualize whatever you want in your mind, you are going to hold it in your hand. Nothing can come into your experience unless you summon it through persistent thoughts. Always be aware of your thoughts.

Look around you. The things you like and the things you dislike you created. Always be sure you are thinking positive thoughts. If we really want to create something and we let negative thoughts creep in then those thoughts negate what was already started.

Sometimes things come as a lesson for us to grow by experiencing and sometimes Spirit has another plan. As an example; I had a friend who was going to give up her job and travel the US for a year. She needed to get away from all the stress she had created. She needed a different car and wanted a good used one and wanted it to be white. She looked and looked and didn't seem to find just what she searched for. One day she saw an orange car, the kind she wanted and everything except for the color but she couldn't refuse the car because of the price. She asked Spirit what that was all about and Spirit said that the car needed to be seen on the road because of the places she would be going. Spirit/God/guides/angels are always with us protecting us and presenting lessons we need to learn.

You draw everything to yourself; the people, job, circumstances, health, wealth, debt, joy, the community you live in. You draw them to you because like attracts like. If you are involved with something or people you'd rather not be, then ask Spirit what you are doing to attract them and then change.

Remember; what we sow we reap!

Do you have people that used to be your good friends but now you find you still love them but there is nothing in common any more? That just means one has outgrown the other and I mean one has more awareness and now you attract different people.

To attract money, focus on wealth. It is impossible to bring money into your life when you focus on the lack of it. Believe you already have the money you want. Always think anything you want you already have. Say "I have" or "I am" as if it is already accomplished. Visualize checks coming in the mail and your bank account having a large sum of money in it. Remember, don't let negative thoughts creep in. Feel grateful and happy to bring positive things into your life.

If you want to attract a relationship make sure your thoughts, words and actions don't contradict your desires. If you feel depressed you block the love and will attract someone that feels the same way. You need to love yourself to attract the same. You can only love someone to the degree you love yourself.

Remember; you can create miracles if you think you can and hold those positive thoughts!

Girls do a technique to discern color by the vibration.

6. OUR SENSES AND MORE

We have always heard of the five senses. Actually, there are many more. We could call a sense of time, tension, pressure, thermoception and others senses. Let's take a look at the senses of hearing, touch, seeing, taste and smell to a deeper level. For this purpose we will group taste and smell together.

We all have all the senses but we have the senses in different orders.

The hearing sense is also known as clairaudient and this person that works more with his hearing picks up an impression and translates into an intellectual understanding. He is direct in his dealings, frank and honest, and an alert mind. He grasps the overall perspective and is more original than conventional. Must understand things before he accepts them and then is a real go-getter and are leaders in society. He is known as an intuitive.

The visionary is also known as clairvoyant. The visionary always translates an impression and thoughts into a mental picture in the mind's eye. They have photographic minds and can recall places, dates, events and names with ease. They are always neat in appearance with every hair in place. Visionaries create a clean and organized environment and are usually artistic. They can become a perfectionist.

The sense of touch we will call the feeling type. This type is also known as the gift of healing. They are concerned with the healing of others and have a lot of power in their hands. They feel the need to always touch/feel everything. They love soft fabrics and petting kittens. Many have a stuffed animal longer than others. They usually have a lot of energy and are outgoing. The feeler type is gifted in psychometry and through the sense of touch can detect the properties of an object.

Here we are going to group the senses of taste and smell/olfactory together and call it prophecy. This type of person is very sensitive and has an inner knowing. They don't know how they know, but through all their senses they know. This type makes an excellent executive and sees the potential in others. They have a strong concern for the future and plans ahead but many times procrastinates. They tend to spread themselves too thin and have many things going all at once. They love to have fun.

I have mentioned a few traits of the four senses in people but of course there are many more and traits that are also out of balance. You can tell the difference in how people walk. The intuitive has a fast pace. The feeler has a slow pace. The visionary looks down and the prophetic looks everywhere except where they are going and many times falls or steps off the sidewalk and stumbles. We could also call these different types of personalities our gifts, the decision-making part of us. Each gift has their strong points and weakness. Each plays an important role in society and deals with the same scenario differently.

We chose our gift order before coming to planet earth to help us achieve what we came to do.

7. REINCARNATION

Science 101 tells us that energy cannot be created or destroyed but it can change form.

A person is basically energy and we do change form. When we are here on planet earth we have a physical body which is composed of things of planet earth. The physical body is an anchor for our soul while here on earth to learn our lessons. When we pass on we leave our body here and the real part of us, the soul, floats out into the universe. It is already predetermined where we go depending on our state of awareness or our consciousness.

This is called "transitioning" because we are just going from one place to another. There is no loss of consciousness and we have done this many times. There is nothing to fear about death because there is no such thing! Yes, you aren't here on planet earth any more but you are in a place where the energy is much less dense.

My husband transitioned four and a half years ago but he has given me permission to write his story about leaving here.

I had always shared a lot with him about different metaphysical things I had discovered. He usually listened but said he really didn't understand. What I had told him about transitioning was that someone would meet him, either his angel, guide or teacher and to go with them to the light. I repeated that just an hour or two before he left.

About three hours after he left I talked with him. These are his words: "It's beautiful here and I am seeing so many people I know from this lifetime and other lifetimes. My friend [angels] came to get me [when he was ready to leave] and said it was time to go and I said I wasn't ready because I didn't want to leave you, and he assured me you would be fine. The minute he touched me my pain left and I feel good and am happy and having a good time".

I have talked with him a few times since and he's always happy. He said he was taking classes on not being so judgmental and he had some dogs he was playing with but didn't have to be responsible for them. He also said next life he was going to be a teacher. He had met with God and God said he did what he came to do and did a great job. He also said he was rather handsome and I asked how old he was and he said thirty-five. He liked it there because everything was up to him as what to do and when. He was playing a lot of golf.

He doesn't visit me much anymore but on occasion when I didn't realize he was around he will set the alarm clock to ring and I have to go shut if off. Once it was in the middle of the night and that's when I told him not to come again and he doesn't that much any more. Of course, he is busy doing "his thing".

That gives you an idea of life in the hereafter. Of course, it depends on the person and what his beliefs are. I talked with my father after he passed and he said to tell everyone that "death" isn't final. He never understood me when i would mention things that seemed "way out" to him and even asked his angel on the other side if I was OK and they assured him I was. I have to mention that he was going to class for an attitude adjustment, which I thought was appropriate. He said next life he was going to be a doctor. I helped my father to the light because when he transitioned he was stuck as he thought "death" was final. He still saw people and interacted with them (of course they weren't aware), therefore he didn't realize he had transitioned.

The one thing you can do to help a loved one after he/she has passed on is when you sends them around is to tell them to look around and find their guide/angel and follow them to the light. You use the words that are familiar to them.

As I said before, where one goes depends on their state of consciousness. Some become earthbound souls, others go to different levels and the levels have many other levels within them. With enough training and awareness you can visit these levels if desired. I believe the only reason to is to help a soul move on to a higher level and to understand the reason they are there.

Remember, like attracts like in all situations.

I would like to share a couple past life times of people I regressed in my own family.

When my grandson was about eight or nine years old he was spending the day with me and I asked him if he'd like to go to a past lifetime and he did. I took him to the deep relaxation stage and began asking him questions. To make a rather long story short, in that lifetime he began when he was about twelve years of age. He saw himself wading across a shallow place in a river and he went to a house and rapped on the door. A woman and child came to the door and he asked if they had any hog meat. I thought he probably had never heard of the term "hog" this lifetime but one reason he may have visited that lifetime is because the child he saw is his second cousin now.

One time I regressed my husband and he went back to a lifetime when he and I were married and lived in Ireland. He was a minister and I was a teacher and taught the peasants how to read. There was a lot more detail he described but it confirmed to me why he liked the Irish Rovers so much. When they were on television every Saturday night he just had to watch. Also once we went to Portland to see their concert at his insistence. He could relate to one of the musicians and just knew he played that instrument that lifetime. Someone even asked me once if he was Irish because she thought he spoke with an Irish brogue.

Sometimes partners redo a lifetime together. We had a contract to finish something that we didn't complete then. I will say, we have completed it now.

Sometimes we meet someone who was well known in another life. I have a friend who is a woman this life but in another life she was Wyatt Earp.

When you are ready to incarnate again you go before a council and they work with you to see what you need to learn and who the parents will be. You choose them and they agree to welcome you. Our parents provide the best situation for us to learn what we need to.

We have one soul and many physical bodies in eternity. We can go as fast or rest as much as we want between lifetimes. Everyone's scenario is different.

Maybe you have an affinity for a certain area in the world, have an interest in a certain culture or a certain time period like the Civil War. Chances are you lived at that time or place. It works the same way with people. When you meet a person you have an affinity for you have known them in a past life. If you meet someone you don't care for or aren't comfortable around then you have known them before. The fun thing is to find out your relationship with them. If you are interested, some people can regress you back to other lifetimes.

It's the same with your children. Many times a child and one parent will bond more with each other. That's because the two have had a lifetime together. Children come in on one parent's vibration. A child usually has been with at least one parent before. This way they feel more comfortable here.

Look at the child prodigies; some play a piano beautifully at the age of four or five. Or can do great things that an adult has been years practicing. When my first cousin was three someone gave him a tin horn and he picked it up and played songs he had heard. He tuned pianos for a living but couldn't read a note of music. This tells me these gifted children had done this in past lifetimes!

Many times a group will incarnate in the same lifetime and become friends again.

You could do a whole study on the subject of reincarnation and keep finding out things you didn't know existed and things that surprise you. If you are reading this book and relate to most of it you are an old soul.

This bird is replenishing his energy by sharing a peanut butter sandwich with my son while sitting on Todd's gloved hand.

8. YOU ARE UNIQUE

We are all unique. We come into planet earth with different talents, gifts and traits. Many were developed last lifetime and past lifetimes. Some come in with a challenge of some kind because they need to learn to overcome it, to learn lessons and possibly for others to learn lessons.

Shakespeare said, "all the world's a stage and we are merely players". How true. We are acting out a part to learn by and help others learn.

There are souls taking a physical body for the first time and souls who have been here many, many times before. I have a daughter who keeps reincarnating here on planet earth over and over because she loves the planet. I can tell many times the souls that come here time and time again because of their love of the earth itself. They usually have a garden and love to dig in the soil. Many souls choose other planets to spend time on. Each planet offers its own lessons and vibration.

I know someone who had a hard time learning in school. After discovering her last lifetime here, she was very intelligent and looked down on others who didn't meet her intellectual standards. She needs to know what it is like to be in the other role that she judged so this is why she chose that certain intelligent level this time.

We often show sympathy for those with a physical handicap but many choose that so let's not judge because we don't know the story behind the handicap.

You may have heard of Indigo Children and Crystal Children. Indigo Children were up to twenty-some years ago until recently. Those born three or four years and now are called Crystal Children. I don't mean all the children but quite a few. I believe they came to change the world.

Indigo children have a feeling of deserving to be here. Self-worth is not an issue. They become frustrated with the systems and see a better way of doing things. They are "system-busters". I have an Indigo granddaughter and I look at how different she seems. She loves the environment and doesn't understand why others don't respect it. No throw-aways for her.

Crystal Children are more highly evolved and have a universal consciousness and communicate telepathically. They sometimes don't start to talk as early as some because they communicate by gestures or other ways. They are highly spiritual.

I often wonder if children today may be born with a technical chip implant. I think this because at the age of seventy-eight I find it difficult in keeping up technically with the young and they learn at a greater rate of speed. I just learn one thing technical and it's obsolete!

9. DIMENSIONS

This is an infinite, never-ending universe.

There are many dimensions of creation. The building blocks of dimensions are the thoughts, feelings and the electro-magnetic energy we emanate to manifest each one.

Currently we are working on five different levels in five dimensions. We have another "us" in each one. We go from one to another all the time and aren't even aware of it and think it's just our thoughts. If you have heard of "walk-ins", this is what it means. Another us can walk in and exchange places by permission. This has happened to me four times this lifetime. I wanted to go to another place for learning, work or helping in some situation or retreat from this dimension for awhile. No one noticed except my dog and he wouldn't come near me for four or five days. He was confused because I looked the same but my energy was different (this is how sensitive animals are).

We are just moving into the fifth dimension. We are going there because planet earth is evolving to that point. Note the sky will be turning green at night. A lot of people have had a difficult time physically, mentally and/or emotionally the past couple of years. Our bodies have been keeping up with the energy of planet earth to be able to stay here with her. Some have chosen to pass on.

Let me explain; some souls pass on because they have completed their blueprint here and some have destroyed their own physical body with their thoughts, feelings or emotions. At this point our bodies are gradually changing from carbon base to crystalline. Each dimension brings its own traits. Each dimension becomes less dense. Planet earth is very dense compared to the higher realms and some people find it difficult to live here and feel they are on a survival trip.

These changes/transitions are not always smooth. Look at the world situation. The leaders can't seem to agree on much and we feel the civil unrest and discontent amongst the masses due to the widespread anxiety about the world conditions. Chaos precedes peace.

As we evolve we grow lighter in spirit as well as our body becomes lighter and different. We will get to a point when we become a manifesting unit and at a point we will recreate a body for ourselves. Of course, this is only possible after one evolves to a high level of consciousness. This involves many lifetimes and experiences in the universe.

You can become a comet, a planet and your consciousness will be the consciousness of the planet. You can be a star, sun or an entire solar system! This doesn't happen all at once and it will be a long time for most. I want to include here that some people who are in physical bodies now didn't need to come to planet earth to learn lessons but were asked by God to come at this time to help hold the light while we are making this transition to the fifth dimension (this is what the 144,000 souls refers to in Revelations).

This lifetime is but the blinking of an eye in eternity.

10. MEDITATION/COMMUNICATION

We have all the answers within. If we want the answers we need to meditate. Meditation needs to be a morning routine. We can set the energy for the day and start out "on the right foot".

There are different ways to meditate. We can listen to soft music or a guided tour and see where you go. Using a mantra helps some people. What we are trying to achieve is to get to a peaceful and comfortable place to listen within. Prayer is asking, meditation is listening.

What I find that works best for me is deep breathing to begin. Always be aware of the breath to take you to a deeper level. You must create a place without interruptions. Put the animals someplace so they are quiet. No loud clocks ticking, and shut off your phone or turn the volume way down. My little Shih Tzu used to get in my lap and meditated with me. He didn't like to be disturbed when I had completed my quiet time.

See yourself being cleansed in some way. Either by swirling a white light around you, standing under a waterfall or in a shower. Do something so you feel centered and relaxed. Ask your source to come in whether you talk to Spirit, God, angels, teachers, guides or the highest vibration to you. Then I ask for a keyword for the day and ask for further understanding if needed. Regroup this word at night. Then ask questions you want to know. Don't get discouraged if at first you don't feel successful. Everything takes practice. Most people can't play a piano unless they practice!

During meditation is a good time to ask if whatever you have planned for the day will work out for you as far as timing etc. Also ask for support for what you are going to do for the day. Listen to yourself and what Spirit has to say. There are other methods of direct communication with Spirit. Some people use a pendulum and you can use your body as a pendulum.

Meditation is where you find your answers and we've all heard its good for our state of mind and our bodies.

Include prayers for yourself, your family, the US and the world situation. Never think you are imposing on Spirit because that is their job and they are learning just as you are.

Always time for socializing!

MISCELLANEOUS TIDBITS

You already have it or you wouldn't recognize it--stop looking for it!

We talk ourselves out of our true feelings of continuity by our intellect.

We have drifted from Mother Nature--where the answers are.

Don't try to prove it; it means you don't believe in yourself!

You will learn lessons! You are enrolled in full-time informal school called life on planet earth. Every person or incident is the "Universal Teacher".

There are no mistakes, only lessons. Growth is a process of experimentation. Failures are as much a part of the process as success.

If you don't learn easy lessons they get harder.

External problems are a reflection of your internal state.

Others are only mirrors to you. What you see in others you have yourself. If you see something in others that irritates you, you have the same thing to some degree. If you see something you admire in others you also have that to some degree. If you see something you recognize and it doesn't bother you, you have overcome it.

Your life is up to you. Lift provides the canvas, you do the painting.

Above all have fun, joy, happiness and laughter!

If you would like to get in touch with Peggy she can be contacted via email at: brlight@roadrunner.com

Ahura Z. Diliiza offers readings, classes and services online and in person through his school, Unicorn Cove School of Metaphysics. For more information and to contact, visit www.unicorn-cove.com.

www.ingramcontent.com/pod-product-compliance
Lightning Source LLC
Chambersburg PA
CBHW072015060426
42446CB00043B/2563